MEXICAN PINATA PARTY

SPANISH CARNIVAL

THE MACMILLAN PICTURE WORDBOOK

Words by Kathleen N. Daly
Pictures by John Wallner

Macmillan Publishing Co., Inc.
New York

Collier Macmillan Publishers
London

Library of Congress Cataloging in Publication Data
Daly, Kathleen N.
The Macmillan picture wordbook.
Summary: Introduces more than 1500 words,
arranged under subjects including houses, mealtime,
trains, playtime, the seashore, outer space, wild
animals, musical instruments, and manners.
1. Vocabulary — Juvenile literature.
[1. Vocabulary]   I. Wallner, John C., ill.   II. Title.
PE1449.D27   428.1   82-6619
ISBN 0-02-725600-6   AACR2

CONTENTS

HOW TO HELP A CHILD

The Macmillan Picture Wordbook is designed to do more than just teach words. As young readers-to-be match pictures with words, they take a first giant step towards learning to read. Leafing through the book provides a combination of fun and achievement. Each page offers entertainment, discovery, and identification. In addition, there are games that can be played with the words and pictures throughout the book. Here are some suggestions:

1. Find the Cat. On almost every page of this book, there is a little cat somewhere in the picture. Sometimes he is nearly hidden, other times he is easy to see, but always he relates to the family of words being introduced.

2. I Spy. As you enjoy the book with the child, take turns saying, "I spy something red," or, "I spy something round," or, "I spy something with four legs." When the child finds the matching picture, point to the word, say it, and ask the child to repeat it. Then change about and let the child be the "spy."

3. A Child's Own Word List. Play "I Spy" with objects in sight of you and the child. Ask the child to try and find pictures of the objects in the Wordbook. If an object is not in this Wordbook, start a personal word list by writing the word down and then searching for a picture of the word in magazines and catalogs. They provide great illustrations for a child's very own book, and it is fun to cut and paste.

4 **I Remember.** Ask the child to remember people, animals, places, and activities that he or she has recently seen. See if the child can find them in the Wordbook. If not, make another entry in the child's own word list. Learning the words to describe a personal experience is exciting and will lead to rewarding language skills.

5 **Grandma's Trunk.** A very unusual grandma is packing her trunk with anything that begins with, say, the letter B. Look through the book and see what begins with B: bear, butter, bed, beads. . . . Nothing is out of bounds for this funny grandma. A variation of this game could have grandma choose one object from each letter of the alphabet.

6 **Learning To Use a Dictionary.** A dictionary is a wordbook in ABC (alphabetical) order. It also explains what a word means. If the child doesn't understand a word, or if he or she would like to know more about it, look it up in a dictionary. Here is a good way to introduce the use of a dictionary: Turn to any page in this book, look at the words, and, with the help of the child, list them in alphabetical order. It is useful to have a separate card for each letter of the alphabet: an A card, a B card, and so on. The alphabet pages of this book (Apple-Pie ABC on pages 78 and 79) will show the child the order of the letters.

Above all, have fun with this book. Let the child go at his or her own pace, either lingering over a page or skimming on to the next one. Gradually, with growing interest and a feeling of success, the child will grasp the connection between the picture and the printed word that goes with it. Now turn the pages and enjoy the thrill of helping the reader-to-be discover a love and appreciation of words that will always be treasured.

Houses

adobe house

Houses are where people live. There are hundreds of different kinds of houses, in towns and cities and in the country, in hot countries and cold countries. What kind of house do you live in?

mobile home

grass hut

Japanese paper house

desert tent

tepee

igloo

underground house

solar house

roof

skylight

antenna

attic

bathroom

window shutters

window box

bedroom

stairs

garage

living room

front door

kitchen

dining room

driveway

bushes

dryer   washing machine

steps

tools

workbench

hot-water tank

grass

furnace   basement

7

BREAKFAST

orange juice
toaster
cup
coffee pot
orange
squeezer
saucer
cat's dish
cream pitcher
cereal
milk
spoon
jam
bowl
egg
bacon
butter
toast
knife
sugar bowl

Mealtimes

You eat breakfast in the morning. Lunch is a meal that you have at noon. In the evening you usually eat the biggest meal of the day, which is dinner. Sometimes it is called supper. Maybe you have a favorite snack in between meals.

LUNCH

peanut butter and jelly sandwich
thermos
lunch box
napkin
cookies
milk
straw
carrot sticks
fork
cottage cheese
paper plate
school books

DINNER

chocolate cake

fried chicken

tray

salad

salad dressing

platter

plate

salt

pepper

rolls

green beans

water

glass

mashed potatoes

fruit

spoon

tablecloth

SNACK TIME

storybook

popcorn

oatmeal cookies

grapes

Bill's Best

cheese

milk

celery sticks

cat snack

9

Delicatessen

Poultry

Meat

Fish

scales

mustard

cake

shopping list

cookies

bread

pie

PICKLES

Canned Goods

stock clerk

TUNA

shopper

shopping bag

Supermarket

The supermarket is a great place to buy food and household supplies (like catnip). Sometimes whole families go shopping together. At the supermarket you often meet your friends.

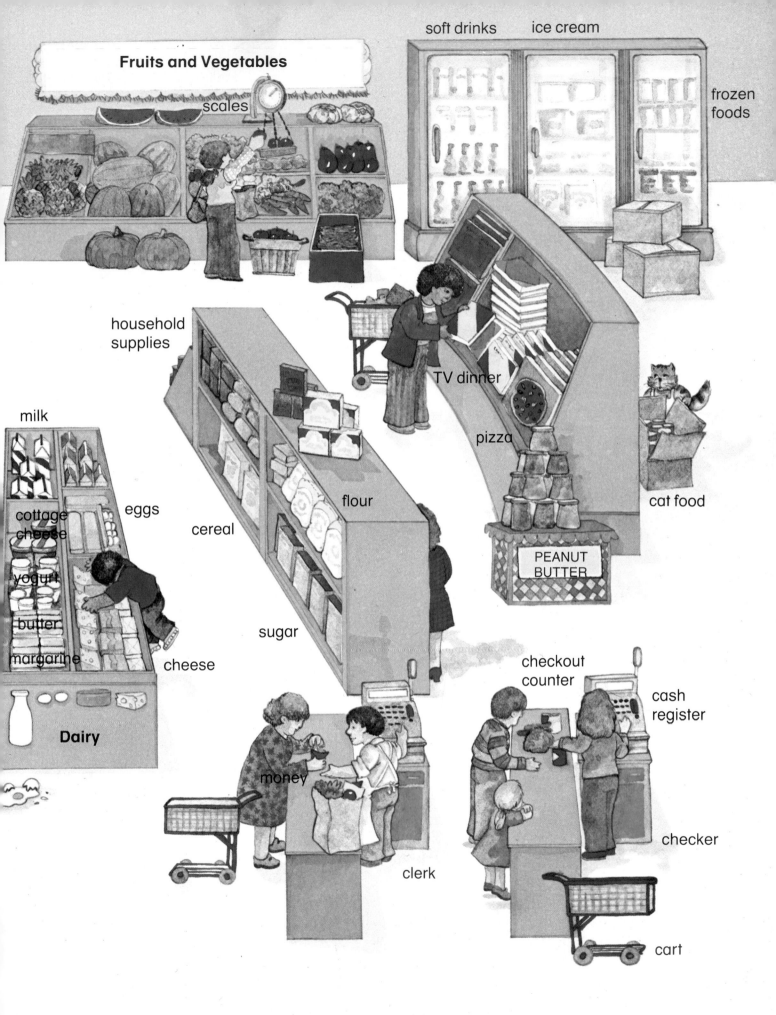

Fruits and Vegetables

scales

soft drinks   ice cream

frozen foods

household supplies

TV dinner

pizza

cat food

milk

cottage cheese

eggs

cereal

flour

yogurt

butter

sugar

margarine

cheese

PEANUT BUTTER

Dairy

checkout counter

cash register

money

clerk

checker

cart

11

butterfly

Spring

Spring is the time for showers and flowers, raincoats and boots, and birds building nests. Nature wakes up from its winter's sleep.

robin

eggs

nest

rainbow

raindrops

sweater

shirt

jumper

overalls

honeybees

sneakers

rain hat

umbrella

raincoat

tulips

puddle

duck

rubber boots

daffodils

pond

tadpoles

ducklings

frog

Summer

Summer is the warmest time of the year. Many people go on vacation in the summer. They may go to the country or to the seashore. They may have picnics in the park. Ants have a wonderful time at picnics.

hammock

fishing pole

cook's hat

canoe

diving board

bathing suit

paddle

inner tube

spatula

sun hat

thermos

T-shirt

sandals

jeans

apron

dragonfly

shorts

caterpillar

lemonade

picnic basket

barbecue

rosebush

fan

ants

ladybug

Fall

As summer ends, days and nights become cooler. In many places leaves change color and fall from the trees. So, people call this season "fall." It's time to go back to school.

geese

branches

falling leaves

cap

rake

sweater

jacket

slacks

shirt

school bag

trousers

pumpkins

apples

rake

pine cone

14

Winter

In many places it snows in winter. It's time for warm clothes. It's time for ice-skating and skiing and building snowmen.

snowflakes

snowmobile

bird feeder

snowman

fir tree

earmuffs

parka

scarf

boots

mittens

ice

sled

puck

hockey stick

snow

gloves

icicle

snowball

ice skates

down jacket

snowsuit

skirt

ski pole

tights

cap

goggles

skis

holly bush

ski boots

15

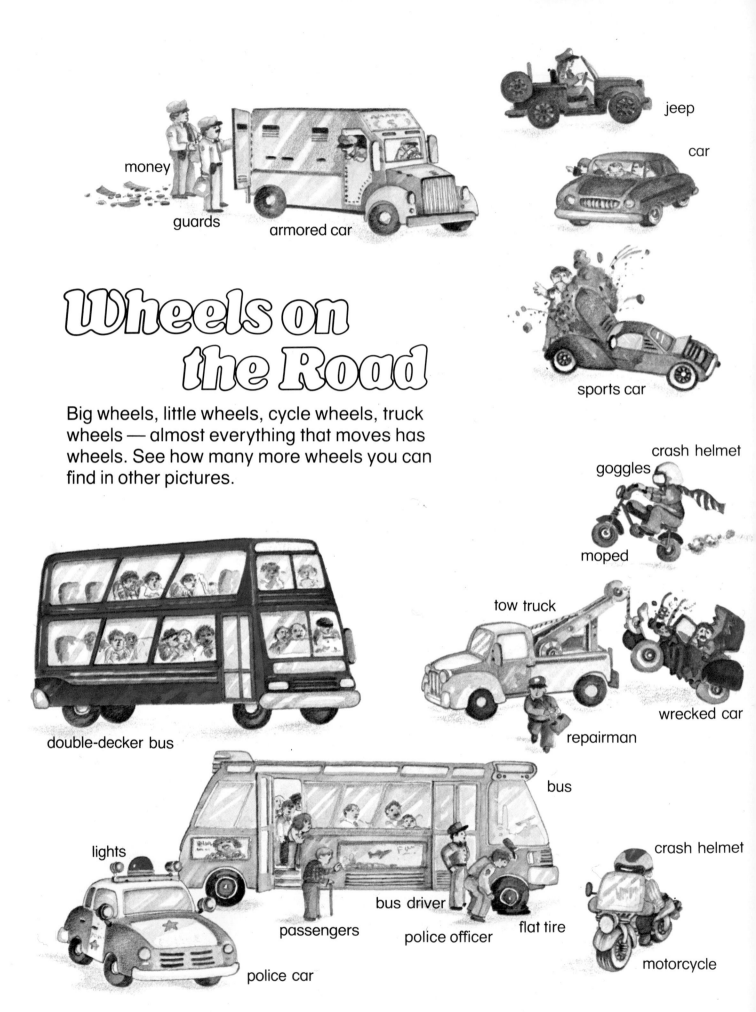

money

guards

armored car

jeep

car

sports car

Wheels on the Road

Big wheels, little wheels, cycle wheels, truck wheels — almost everything that moves has wheels. See how many more wheels you can find in other pictures.

crash helmet

goggles

moped

tow truck

wrecked car

repairman

bus

double-decker bus

lights

crash helmet

passengers

bus driver

police officer

flat tire

motorcycle

police car

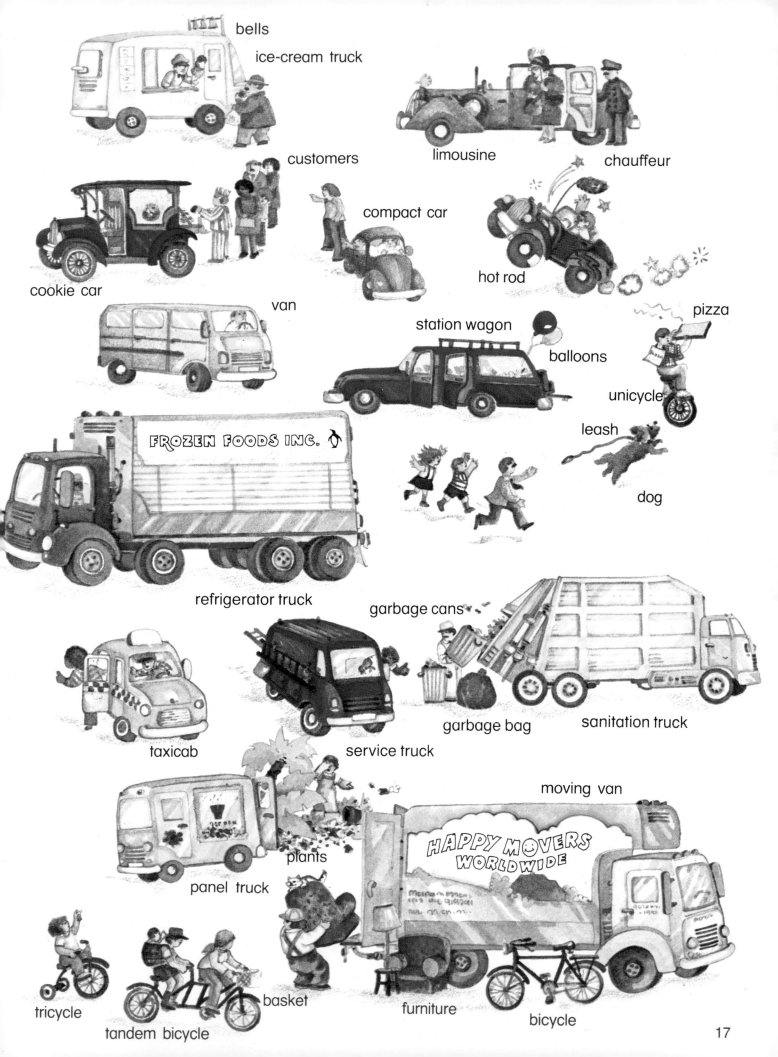

bells

ice-cream truck

customers

limousine

chauffeur

cookie car

compact car

hot rod

van

station wagon

balloons

pizza

unicycle

leash

dog

FROZEN FOODS INC.

refrigerator truck

garbage cans

garbage bag

sanitation truck

taxicab

service truck

moving van

HAPPY MOVERS WORLDWIDE

plants

panel truck

tricycle

basket

furniture

bicycle

tandem bicycle

17

Caterpillar tractor

earthmover

bulldozer

ditchdigger

road grader

dump truck

concrete spreader

surveyor

strike-off board

cement mixer

18

More Wheels

Before wheels can get rolling, people and machines must build roads and highways. It takes many busy people to keep roads in good shape. Look for more wheels in this book. There are lots.

guard rail

FRESH *Daisy* *Dairy* MILK

tank trailer

highway light

Soft Shoulder

cherry picker

road

road cap

car transporter

Ace Gravel Co.

dump truck

road barrier

repair truck

road roller

lumber

scaffold

girder

apartment building

blowtorch

welder

beam

guard

crane

fence

CONSTRUCTION DANGER

street
lamp

excavation

traffic
light

sidewalk

DALY'S DEPARTM

hard hat

cables

sewer
pipes

MEN
AT
WORK

WALK

TELEPHONE

SUBWAY

workers

ramp

window-shoppers

cement mixer

tunnel

SUBWAY

EXPRESS

stairs

turnstile

20

The City

A city is an exciting place. Here, thousands of people live and work day and night. Other people visit a city to see the big buildings, to enjoy themselves, and to do business. Many stop to watch a skyscraper being built.

police officer

office building

bus

police officer

Cafe

CINEMA

TICKETS

ANTIQUES

ORE

Newsstand

DRESSES

BUS STOP

parking meter

fire hydrant

MEN WORKING

manhole cover

manhole

subway train

hot-dog cart

mailbox

MAIL

spire

rose window

cathedral

temple

Alex's

restaurant

steeple

bell tower

church

stained-glass window

museum

TOYS

store

minaret

dome

balcony

apartment building

mosque

synagogue

stadium

skyscraper

library

POST OFFICE

post office

LIBRARY

Buildings

Your house is a building that is special to you.
There are other special buildings. They are
places where people work, read, learn, play,
eat, and worship. Look for more buildings in
this book.

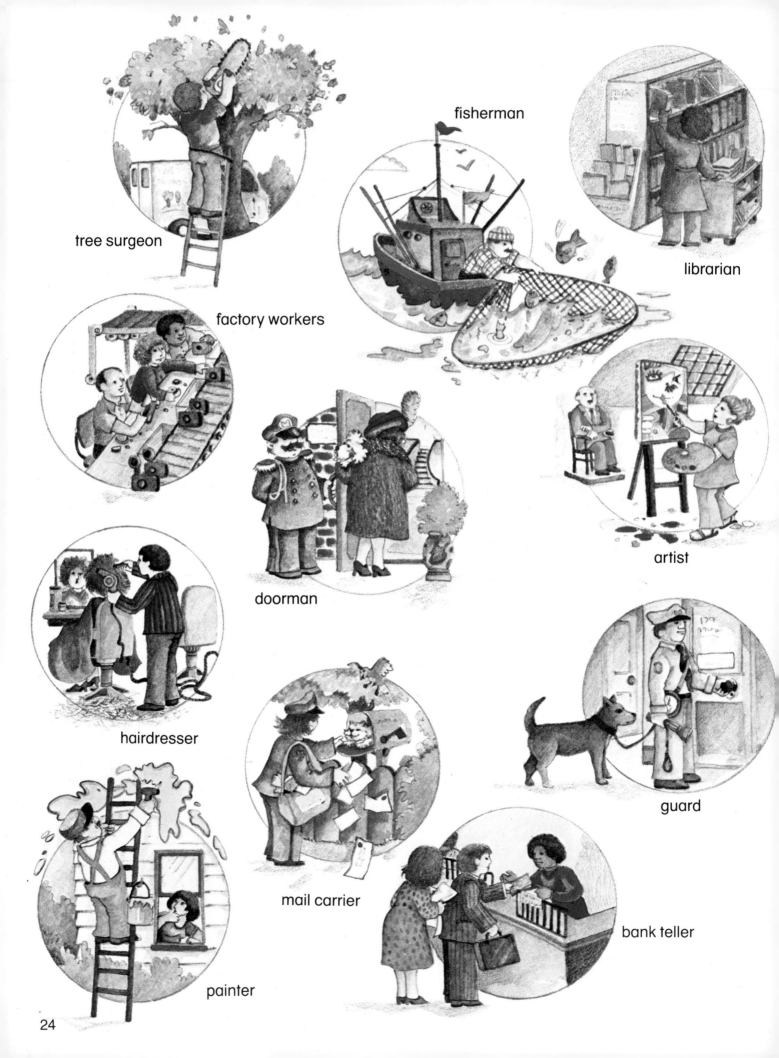

tree surgeon

fisherman

librarian

factory workers

doorman

artist

hairdresser

mail carrier

guard

painter

bank teller

24

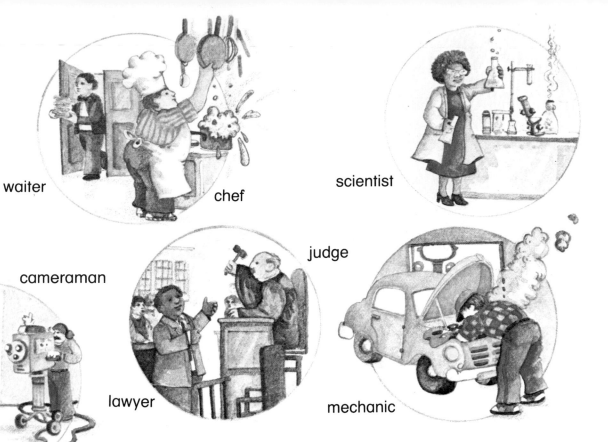

waiter

chef

scientist

cameraman

judge

lawyer

mechanic

newscaster

computer operator

People at Work

Here are some people working at their occupations. There are many other jobs that people do. You can find some of them in this book. What do you dream of doing when you grow up?

plumber

salesperson

miner

factory

container

warehouse

container ship

tugboat

motorboat

tugboat

crane

pulleys

sailor

cargo

life preserver

S.S.SEACAT

hold

bow (front)

anchor

dock

harbor master

cargo

26

Ships and Boats

Ships and boats go to places called ports. In the harbor and on the dock you can see busy people. Which person would you like to be?

tanker

ferryboat

towline

foghorn

barge

coast guard cutter

wreck

smokestack

radar antenna

captain's bridge

lifeboats

stern (back)

deck

cook

portholes

cargo ship

net

gangplank

forklift truck

wind speed gauge

parachute

windsock

radar scanner

restaurant

runway lights

control tower

observation deck

FOOD

parking lot

CAR RENTAL

The Airport

An airport is a place where all kinds of airplanes take off and land on the runways. Some carry cargo. Many of them carry hundreds of passengers. Small airplanes may hold only two people. Have you ever gone to an airport?

EXIT ENTRANCE

SHOPS

CHECK-IN

ARRIVAL

DEPARTURE

tickets

LUGGAGE

porter

baggage cart

INFORMATION

automatic doors

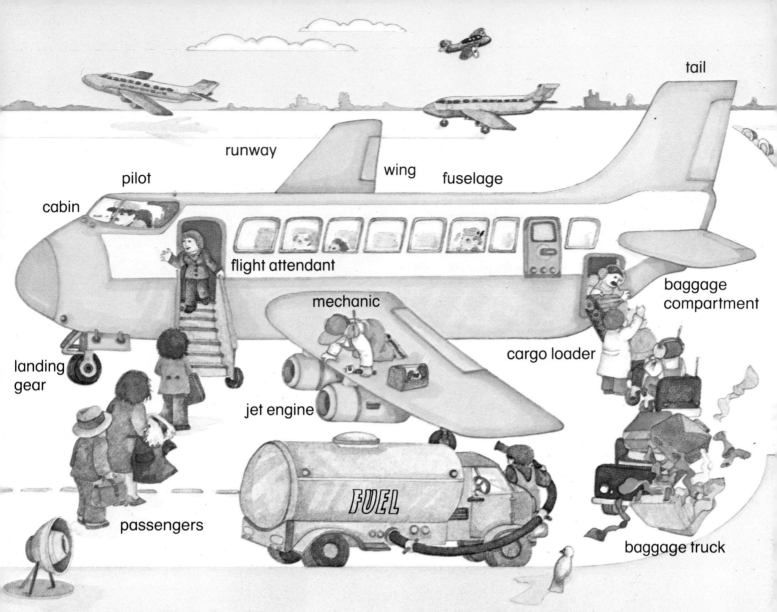

tail

runway

pilot

wing   fuselage

cabin

flight attendant

baggage
compartment

mechanic

cargo loader

landing
gear

jet engine

passengers

FUEL

baggage truck

public address system

newsstand   restrooms   telephones   gates

MEN   WOMEN

water
fountain

GATE 16   GATE 17

security check

waiting room

29

Trains

Long before there were airplanes or buses, trains carried people and freight along hundreds of miles of railroad tracks across the country. The locomotive pulled the train of cars through tunnels in the mountains and across bridges over the rivers.

caboose

tunnel

crossing gate

crossing signal

railroad crossing

signal tower

switch box

diesel locomotive

conductor

flatcar

timber

coupling

tank car

boxcar

girder

trestle bridge

smoke

station

GREYWOOD

Waiting Room

Tickets

engineer

station master

platform

fender

steam locomotive

passengers

railroad tracks

ties

passenger car

School

You go to school to learn all kinds of things: reading, writing, spelling, drawing, music. You learn how to take care of animals. And you learn to play games and make friends with other children.

piano

goldfish

songbook

guitar

baton

record player

Music Corner

record albums

Quiet Corner

hand bells

tambourine

pillow

teacher

drum

blanket

drumsticks

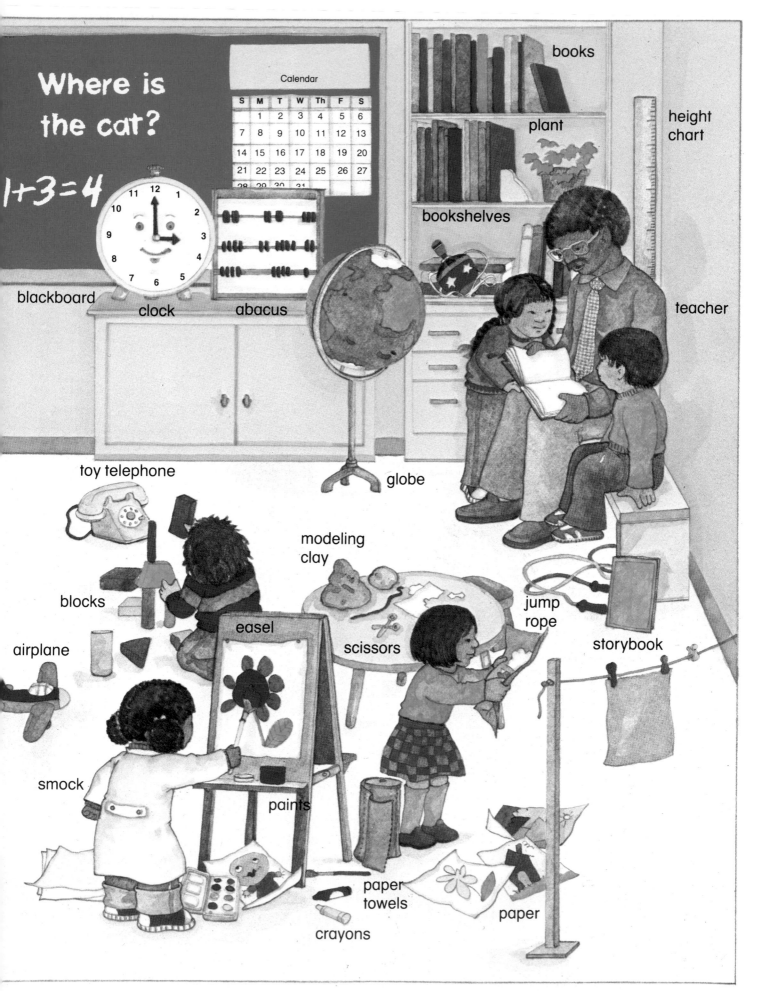

Where is the cat?

1+3=4

Calendar

S	M	T	W	Th	F	S
		1	2	3	4	5	6
7	8	9	10	11	12	13
14	15	16	17	18	19	20
21	22	23	24	25	26	27
28	29	30	31			

books

plant

height chart

bookshelves

teacher

blackboard

clock

abacus

globe

toy telephone

modeling clay

jump rope

blocks

storybook

easel

airplane

scissors

smock

paints

paper towels

paper

crayons

33

hand puppet

airplane

balloons

books

Playtime

Playtime is when you do things just for fun. Some people like to run around and make a noise. Some like quiet games. Some like to read or to draw. What would you do if you lived in this "playtime" picture?

coloring book

toy chest

checkers

crayons

marbles

checkerboard

jump rope

easel

soap bubbles

teddy bear

electric train

pull toy

robot

building toy

remote control

dollhouse

kite

mirror

doll

dress-up
clothes

doll furniture

tricycle

car

blocks

outer-space doll

jigsaw
puzzle

boa

tracks

roller
skates

collections

Rocks

Shells

car

Sports

Sports are games that we play. People everywhere enjoy playing and watching sports. They can go to see them "live," or they can watch them on television.

stadium

helmet

shoulder pad

face guard

football

referee

cheer leaders

players

goal post

knee pad

FOOTBALL

thigh pad

hip pad

cleated shoes

backboard

scoreboard

hoop

basketball

net

BASKETBALL

coach

referee

1st base

36

umpire

racket

TENNIS

ball

net

lines

tennis court

soccer ball

net

SOCCER

goal

players

field

stadium

umpire

bat

batter

ball

mitt

cap

mask

chest
protector

catcher

shin
guards

home
plate

3rd base

pitcher

2nd base

BASEBALL

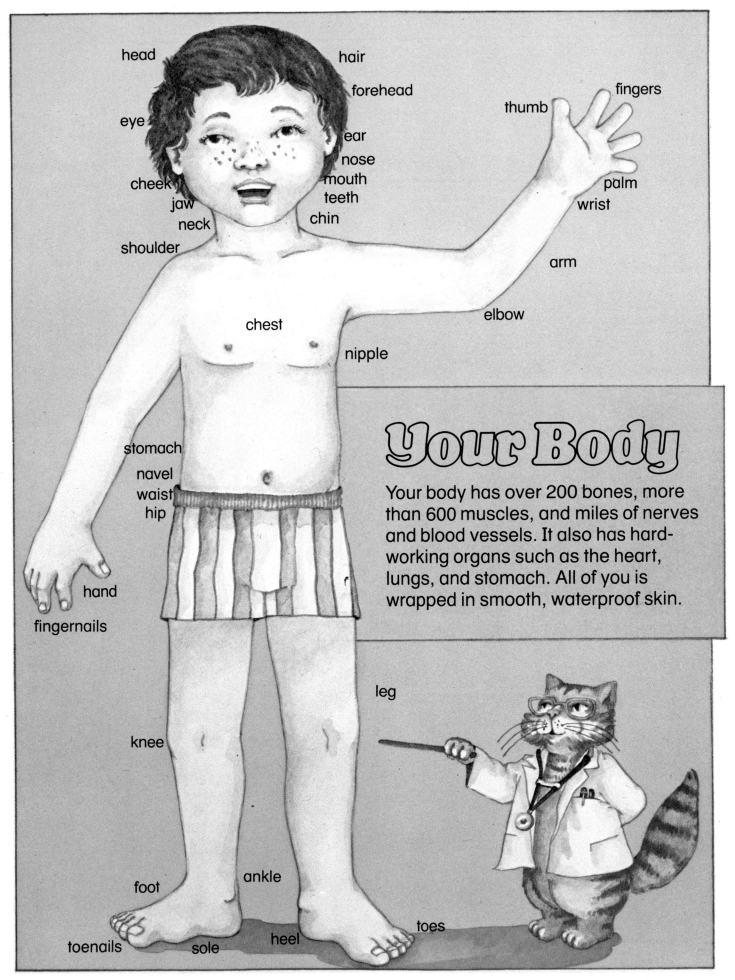

Your Body

Your body has over 200 bones, more than 600 muscles, and miles of nerves and blood vessels. It also has hard-working organs such as the heart, lungs, and stomach. All of you is wrapped in smooth, waterproof skin.

head
hair
forehead
fingers
thumb
eye
ear
nose
palm
mouth
teeth
wrist
cheek
jaw
chin
neck
shoulder
arm
elbow
chest
nipple
stomach
navel
waist
hip
hand
fingernails
leg
knee
ankle
foot
toes
toenails
sole
heel

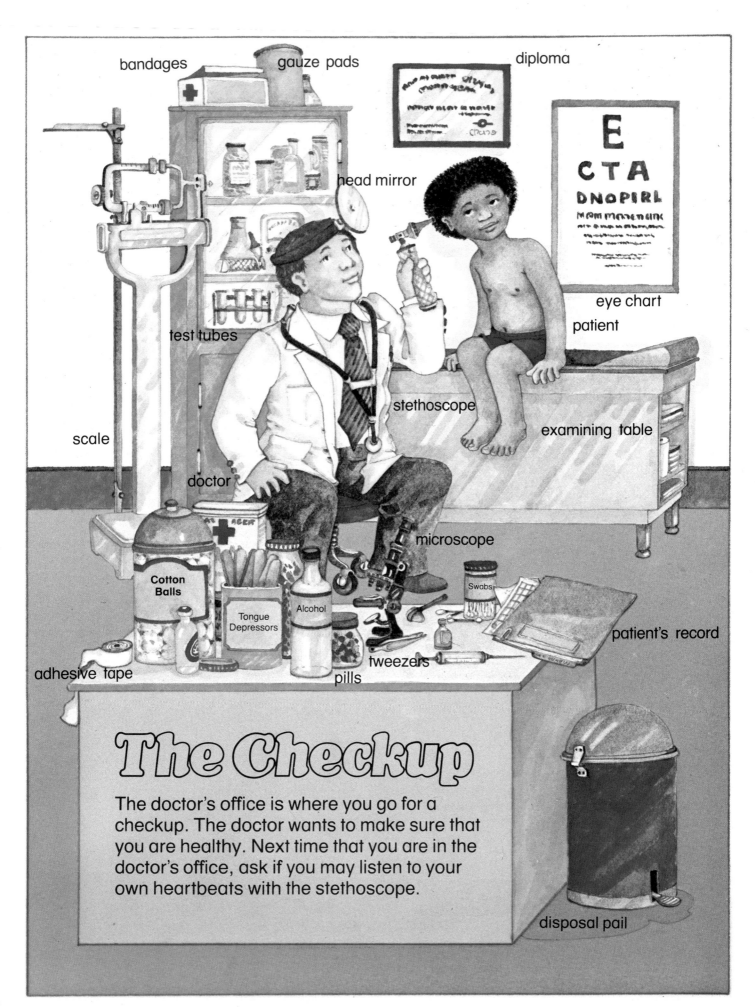

bandages

gauze pads

diploma

head mirror

test tubes

scale

doctor

eye chart

patient

stethoscope

examining table

microscope

Cotton Balls

Tongue Depressors

Alcohol

Swabs

patient's record

adhesive tape

tweezers

pills

The Checkup

The doctor's office is where you go for a checkup. The doctor wants to make sure that you are healthy. Next time that you are in the doctor's office, ask if you may listen to your own heartbeats with the stethoscope.

disposal pail

aunt

uncle

mother

father

parakeet

dog

photographer

camera

grandmother

grandfather

sister

puppies

The Family and Its Pets

This family and some of its pets are having a picture taken. Oh, my! Look what else is happening.

tripod

kittens

frog

teddy bear

mobile

cousins

baby carriage

cousin

playpen

goldfish

brother

hamster

stroller

baby

turtle

bib

diaper

bottle

rattle

bootees

41

The Countryside

The countryside is a great place for vacations, fishing, and having picnics. Farmers live and work there, too. Take a walk in the country. Walk softly and look carefully. You will see birds and many other animals, as well as flowers and trees.

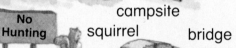

trees

waterfall

forest

sailboat

lake

picnic table

campsite

No Hunting

squirrel

bridge

bird

stream

WILDLIFE PRESERVE

backpack

fishing pole

hiker

canteen

woodland trail

walking stick

flowers

hiking boots

mountain

farm

tollbooth

bridge

river

highway

roadside stand

MOTEL

parking lot

bushes

skunk

binoculars

rowboat

birdwatcher

campfire

tent

43

windmill

weather vane

apple orchard

field

beehives

farmhouse

billy goat

pump

rocking chair

nanny goat

kid

porch

vegetable garden

rake

mailbox

dog

hay bales

stone wall

pickup truck

The Farm

The farmer and his wife, the children, and the farmhands are all kept busy taking care of the crops and the animals on the farm. Even the cat may get up to chase away the mice—when he is not too busy sleeping.

geese

crows

scarecrow

silo

lightning rod

pasture

toolbox

ducks

farmhand

meadow

sheep

pond

hayloft

safety glasses

ladder

barn

horse

chain saw

plow

farmer

water trough

calf

tractor

cows

pail

hens

piglets

mud

chicks

pigs

pigpen

rooster

The Ranch

A ranch is a very large farm where cattle, horses, or sheep are raised. Sometimes helicopters help the cowboys at round-up time when the herds are brought in to be checked and branded.

cowboy

windmill

mesa

bunkhouse

bandanna

mane

horse

ten-gallon hat

vest

quirt

saddle

blanket

bridle

bit

reins

chaps

spur

stirrup

boots

cactus

hoof

helicopter

desert

jeep

lasso

O·CAT·CORRAL

barbed-wire fence

cattle herd

steer

calf

branding iron

jeans

fire

47

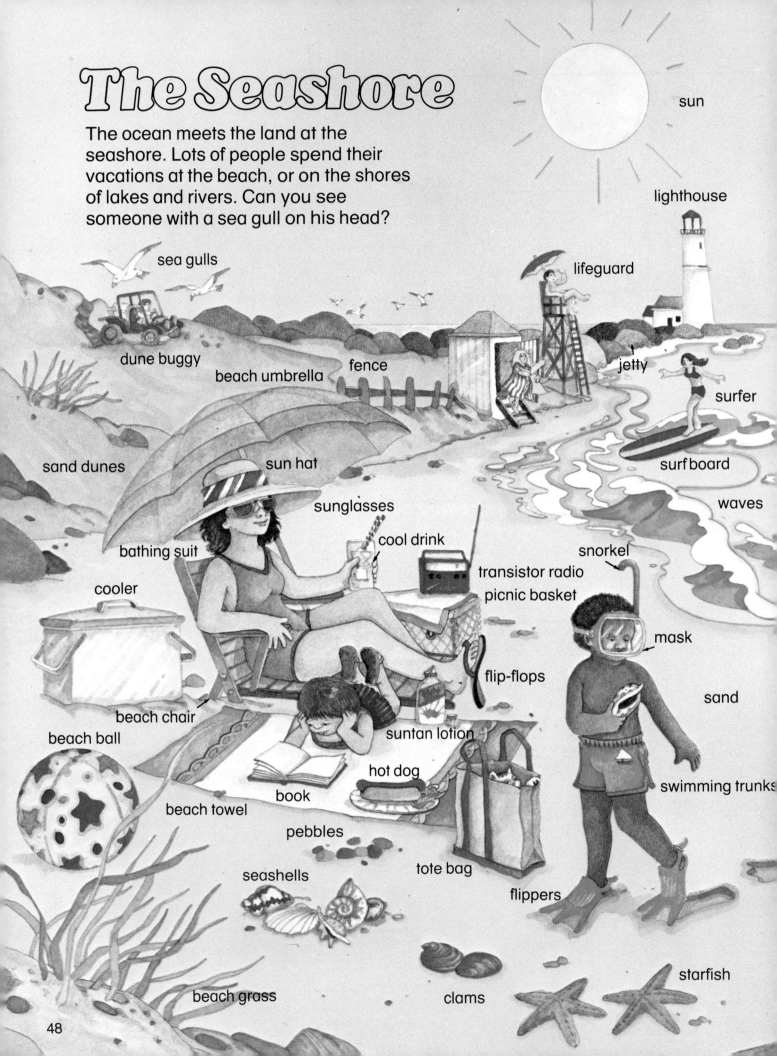

The Seashore

The ocean meets the land at the seashore. Lots of people spend their vacations at the beach, or on the shores of lakes and rivers. Can you see someone with a sea gull on his head?

sun

lighthouse

sea gulls

lifeguard

dune buggy

fence

jetty

beach umbrella

surfer

sand dunes

sun hat

surfboard

waves

sunglasses

cool drink

snorkel

bathing suit

transistor radio

picnic basket

mask

cooler

flip-flops

sand

beach chair

suntan lotion

beach ball

hot dog

swimming trunks

book

beach towel

pebbles

tote bag

seashells

flippers

starfish

beach grass

clams

48

Outer Space

The galaxy in which we earthlings and cat-lings live is full of wonderful things: planets, moons, and stars, comets and meteors, spacecraft and artificial satellites. Astronauts are the explorers of our galaxy. Perhaps you may shuttle off into space one day!

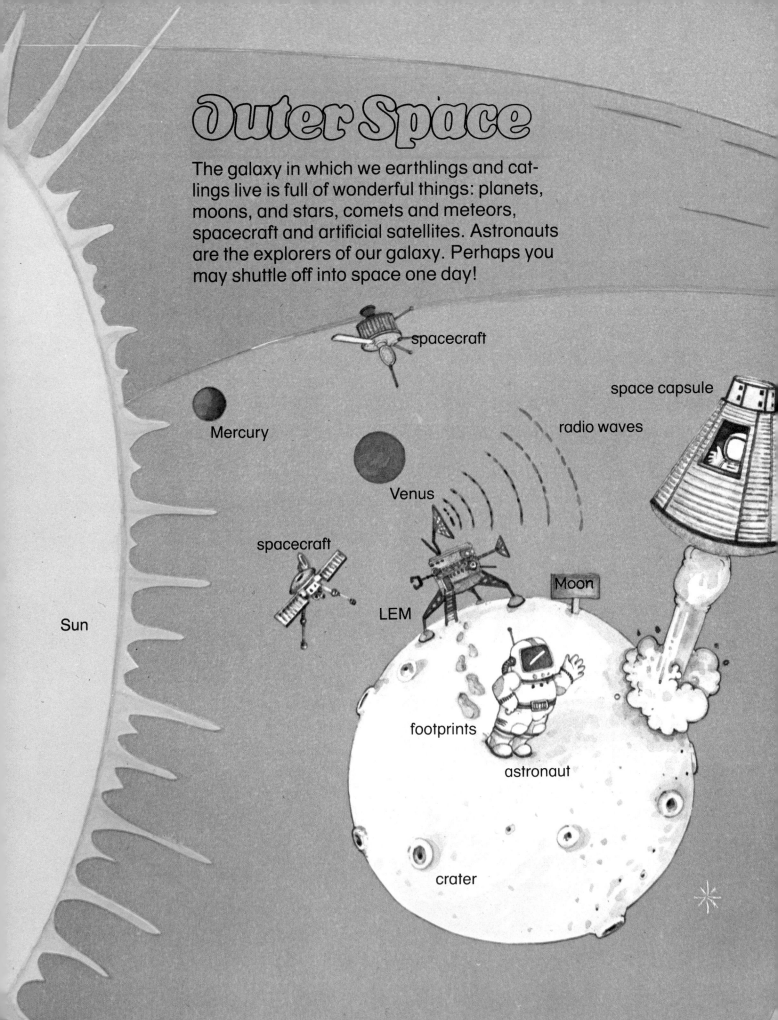

spacecraft

space capsule

Mercury

radio waves

Venus

spacecraft

Moon

LEM

footprints

astronaut

Sun

crater

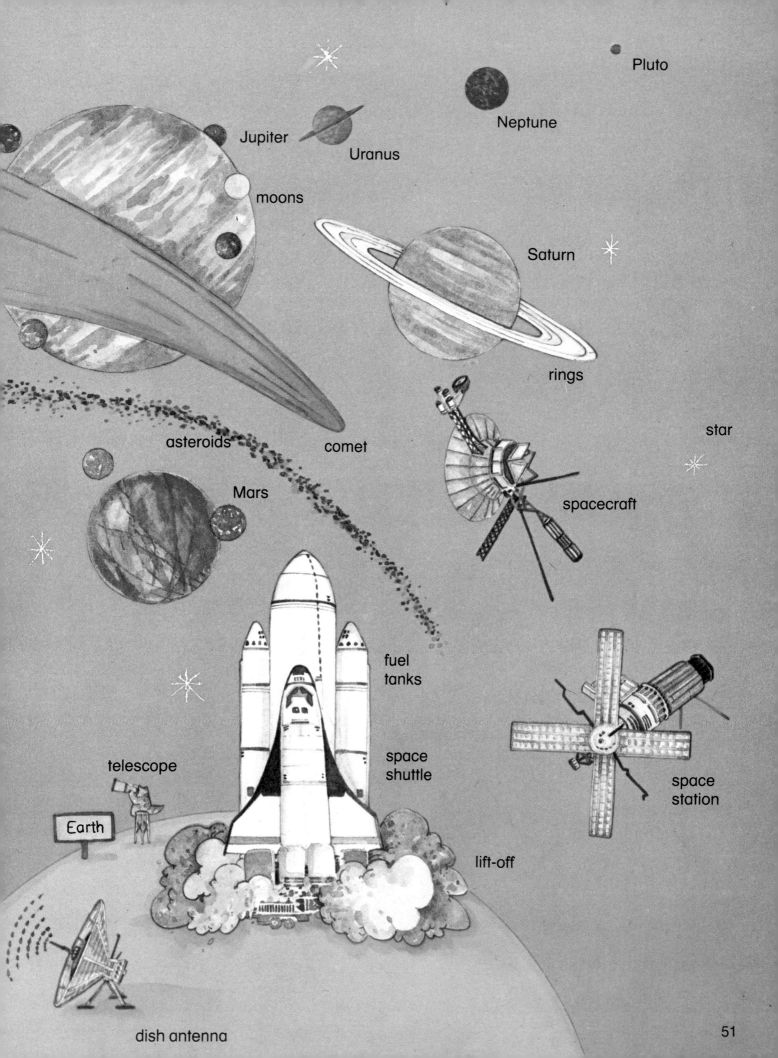

Pluto

Neptune

Jupiter

Uranus

moons

Saturn

rings

star

asteroids

comet

spacecraft

Mars

fuel
tanks

space
shuttle

telescope

Earth

space
station

lift-off

dish antenna

Firefighters

Brave firefighters have come to the rescue. That lady on the roof is going to get wet, but she will be saved. Can you see anyone else who needs help?

smoke

fire chief

two-way radio

light

fire hydrant

bell

nozzle

fire chief's car

pumper

firefighter

hose

hose

stretcher

ambulance

firefighter's helmet

bullhorn

barrier

hose

motorcycle

boots

policeman

fire alarm box

smoke

chimney

ax

firefighter

gas mask

oxygen tanks

firefighter

water

fire

rescue net

hose

ladder

ax

light

hook-and-ladder truck

firefighter

STOP

crossing guard

puddle

fire hydrant

53

koala

kangaroo

joey

panda

grizzly bear

Wild Animals

Wild animals do not usually live with people. Some of these animals have come from faraway places. Others may live next door to you in the fields and woods. See how many other animals you can find in this book.

antlers

brown bear

moose

porcupine

deer

fawn

fox

raccoon

squirrel

snake

rhinoceros

tiger

giraffe

elephant

lion

zebra

frog

monkey

gorilla

hippopotamus

alligator

osprey

blue jay

robin

flock of geese

hawk

crow

oriole

owl

eagle

cardinals

tanager

starling

Canada goose

heron

pelican

flamingo

roadrunner

gosling

spoonbill

cattails

swan

cygnets

duck

56

mourning
dove

Birds

Birds come in all sizes, from the tiny, jewel-like hummingbird to the mighty eagle. All birds have feathers and most of them fly. They live in woodlands and prairies, on mountains, in jungles and deserts, and even in cities. Baby birds hatch from eggs that the mother bird lays in a nest.

sparrow

woodpecker

goldfinch

meadowlark

pheasant

peacock

swift

hummingbird

parakeet

ibis

bird of
paradise

parrot

toucan

cockroach

cricket

branch

Plants and Insects

Plants grow from seeds. Trees are the biggest plants of all. Honeybees and other insects carry pollen from one flower to another so that more plants may grow. All insects hatch from tiny eggs. Did you know that caterpillars turn into beautiful butterflies and moths?

dragonfly

housefly

mosquito

rose

poppy

firefly

petals

daisy

butterfly

stem

leaves

thorn

ants

dandelion

bud

violet

mushrooms

cactus

clover

grasshopper

moss

grass

wasp

honeybee

caterpillar

tree
trunk

butterfly

bumblebee

beetle

moth

buttercup

ladybug

praying
mantis

black-eyed
Susan

fern

walking
stick

ivy

branch

spider web

wooly bear

roots

spider

59

Sea Animals

There are thousands of fish and other animals in the ocean. Did you know that the blue whale is the biggest animal that has ever lived? Whales and dolphins are not fish. They have to come up for air. Scuba divers carry air tanks on their backs. Can you see a scuba diver?

flying fish

fins

gills

manta ray

shark

tentacles

octopus

school of sardines

eel

suckers

jellyfish

sea horses

dolphin

baby dolphin

coral

swordfish

seal

walrus

penguins

ice floe

baby seal

tunas

sea turtle

flippers

whale

61

brontosaurus

tyrannosaurus

trachodon

ornitholestes

stegosaurus

visitors

spiky tail

pterodactyl

footprints

skeleton

museum worker

saber-toothed tiger
and cub

ladder

triceratops

Dinosaurs
(And Other Animals of Long Ago)

Dinosaurs are the reptiles that lived on earth
millions of years ago. Many of them were
giants, bigger than buses! You may have seen
their bones and footprints in a museum.

baby pterodactyl

eggs

Keeping in Touch

There are many ways to "keep in touch." You can write a letter, send a postcard, and call by telephone. Television, movies, and radio also keep us in touch. Don't forget newspapers, magazines, and books.

typewriter

desk

author

wastepaper basket

OPERATORS

telephone

telephone switchboard

postcard

mail carrier

writer

envelope

stamp

mail cart

BOOKSTORE

books

newspapers

magazines

reader

Hello! I feel better.

mailbox

letter

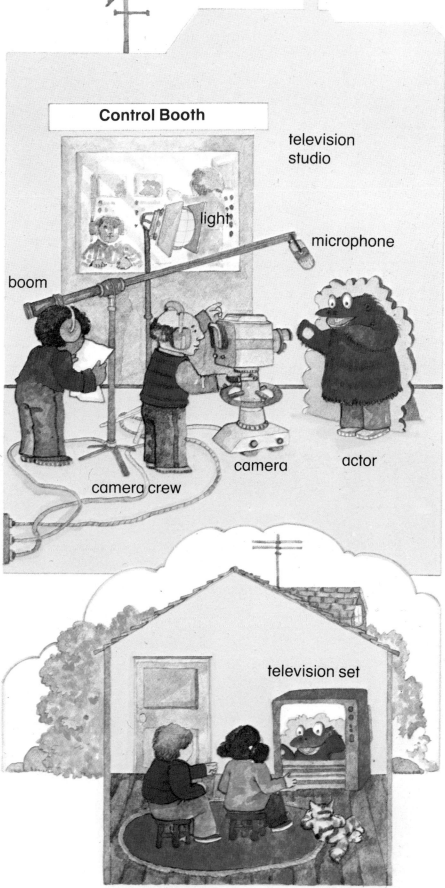

Control Booth

television studio

light

microphone

boom

camera crew

camera

actor

television set

Make-Believe

In the world of make-believe anything can happen. Look at the picture. You may find some old friends you have met in storybooks. You may meet some new friends. Can you find the end of the sea monster's tail?

witch

broomstick

ghost

spaceman

flying saucer

pirate flag

crow's-nest

wings

smoke

horns

sails

pirate

dragon

collar

cannon

anchor

galleon

leash

treasure chest

parrot

rowboat

brownies

claws

mouse

wings

fairy

toadstool

pipe

goblin

elf

snail

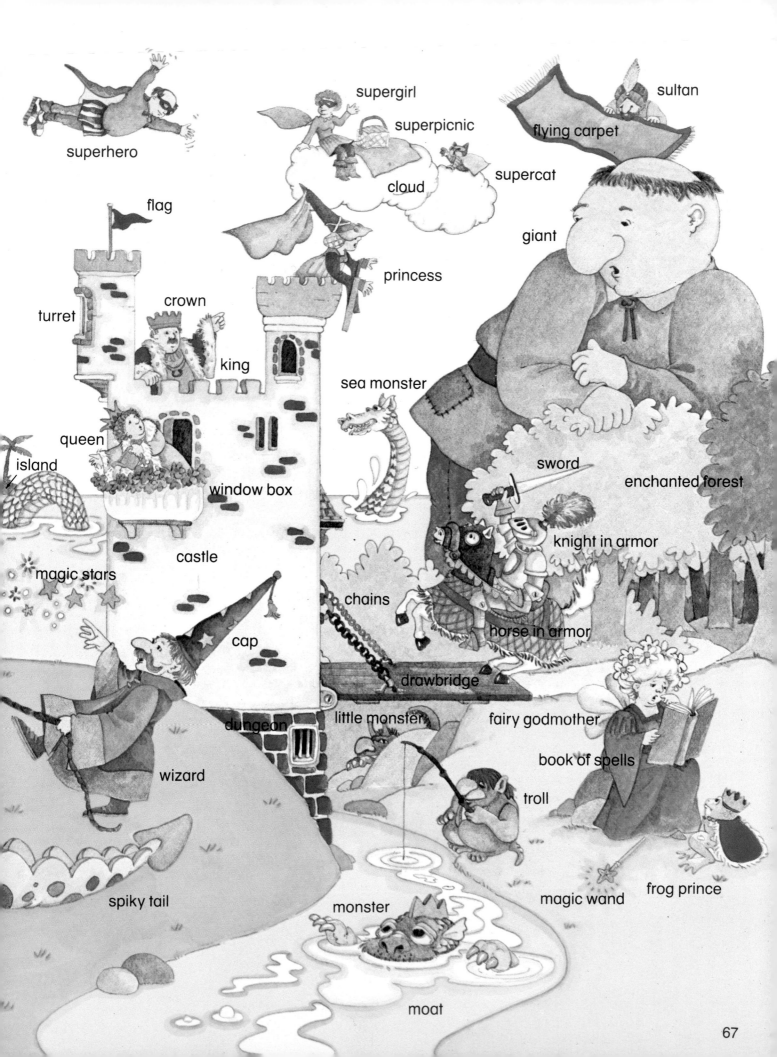

superhero

supergirl

superpicnic

supercat

cloud

sultan

flying carpet

giant

flag

turret

crown

king

princess

queen

island

window box

sea monster

sword

enchanted forest

knight in armor

castle

magic stars

chains

horse in armor

cap

drawbridge

wizard

dungeon

little monster

fairy godmother

book of spells

troll

spiky tail

monster

magic wand

frog prince

moat

Counting

At last all the cats in the book have come out of hiding. Each one is wearing a number on its T-shirt. Can you count the cats from one to ten?

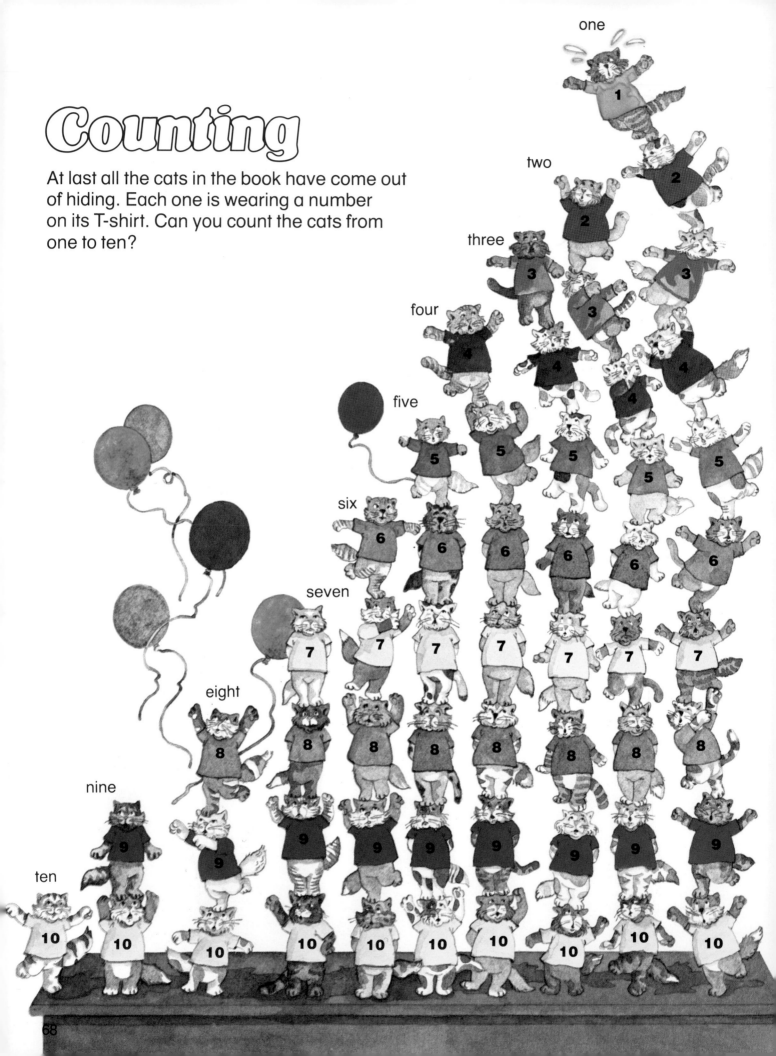

one

two

three

four

five

six

seven

eight

nine

ten

Telling Time

minute hand

hour hand

clock

When the sun comes up, it's morning. It's time to get up! Clocks and watches tell us what time it is. Which time do you like best: getting-up time, lunch time, or going-to-bed time? Cats like catnap time.

GOING-TO-SCHOOL TIME

tower clock

SCHOOL

GETTING-UP TIME

alarm clock

LUNCH TIME

electric clock

wristwatch

BATHTIME

grandfather clock

digital clock

STORY TIME

BEDTIME

69

diamond

crescent

circle

cone

oval

sphere

rectangle

pyramid

star

cube

triangle

Shapes

Everything around you has some kind of a shape. Is your window a square or a rectangle? Can you see a crescent moon, or a round moon? Be sure to wish upon a ☆!

square

heart

purple

orange

green

red

paintbrush

brown

white

blue

yellow

black

Colors

Colors are all around you. When you mix paints together you can make new colors. What happens if you mix blue and yellow? What is your favorite color?

short

tall

small

THIN

big

happy

open shut

sad

DOWN

UP

UPSIDE DOWN

RIGHT SIDE UP

on

off

FAT

Opposites

When things are completely different from each other, we say they are opposites. Black is the opposite of white. Good is the opposite of bad. This funny circus shows lots of opposites. See how many more you can think of.

pull

push

Signs

Signs help us to find things and places.
They help us to watch out for danger, too.
Look for other signs in this book.

Tools

file

pliers

Tools are objects that people have made to help them in their work or in their hobbies. Here are tools to use in the house and tools to use outdoors. See how many tools you can find on other pages.

sandpaper

folding ruler

chisel

plane

screwdriver

bolt

drill

screws

nuts

nails

hammer

wrench

coping saw

harp

recorder

harmonica

clarinet

accordion

trumpet

bagpipe

violin

French horn

bugle

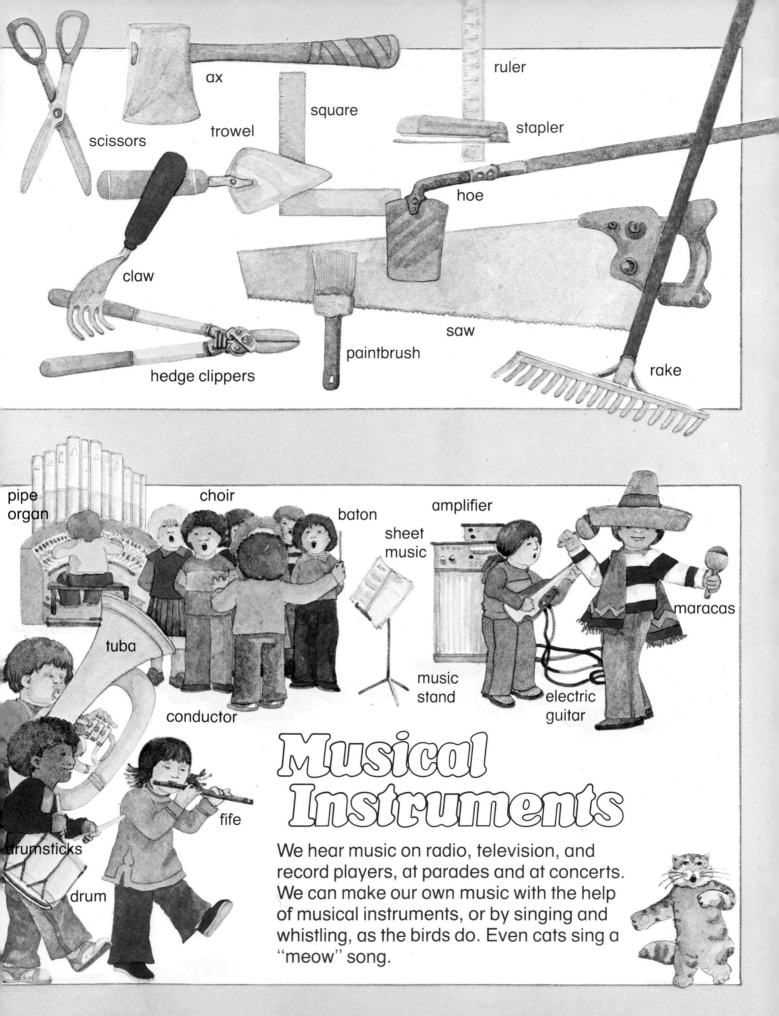

scissors

ax

trowel

square

ruler

stapler

hoe

claw

saw

paintbrush

hedge clippers

rake

pipe organ

choir

baton

amplifier

sheet music

tuba

maracas

music stand

electric guitar

conductor

fife

drumsticks

drum

Musical Instruments

We hear music on radio, television, and record players, at parades and at concerts. We can make our own music with the help of musical instruments, or by singing and whistling, as the birds do. Even cats sing a "meow" song.

Manners

Having good manners is being polite. The opposite of polite is rude and not caring at all about how another person feels. Aren't you glad your good manners help make life easier and more pleasant for everyone you know?

Please come to my party.

Thanks. I'd love to.

Good morning.

Hello.

Hi!

How do you do?

I'm very glad to meet you.

Have a nice day!

Thank you.

77

Apple-Pie ABC

Here is a story about an apple pie and the 26 letters of the alphabet. Try making up your own story, using each letter from A to Z.

Aa

A was an apple pie.

Ee

Elephant eyed it.

Ff

Fox fled with it.

Gg

Gorilla grabbed it back.

Kk

Koala kissed it.

Ll

Lion looked after it.

Mm

Monkey marched to the table with it.

Qq

Quail quartered it.

Rr

Rhinoceros roared for it.

Ss

Snake sat down for a bite.

Ww

Walrus wept for it.

Xx

Xenops x-rayed it.

Yy

Yak yelled yum-yum for it.

Bb Bear baked it.

Cc Cat clawed it.

Dd Dog dreamed about it.

Hh Hippopotamus held onto it.

Ii Inchworm inched around it.

Jj Jaguar jumped for it.

Nn Nanny goat nibbled at it.

Oo Ostrich observed it.

Pp Pig peeped at it.

Tt Tiger tasted it, too.

Uu Unicorn upset it.

Vv Vole viewed it.

Zz Zebra zoomed in and ate the rest of it.

The End And that was the end of the apple pie.

Good Night!

Night is the time when most people and animals sleep. But some people, such as bakers and night watchmen, are at work. And some animals leave their babies in their cozy homes and go out hunting for food.

fox

garbage can

birds

raccoons

nest

tree hollow

rabbits

kittens

doghouse

basket

cat

dog   puppies

good night

lamp

child   bed

slippers

SPRING

FIREWORKS

CHINESE NEW YEAR